Leadership Perspectives

Practice Competency Insights for Leadership Evolution in Business

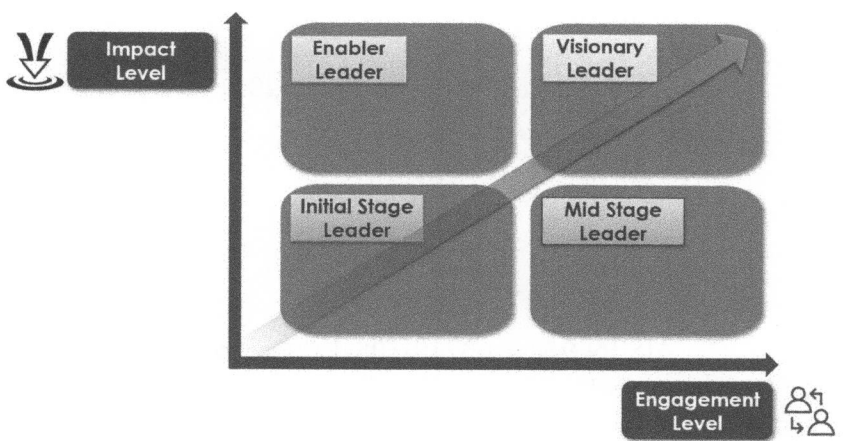

Sundar Ananthasivan

A Phased Reflective Leadership Approach

Fulton Books, Inc.
Meadville, PA

Published by Fulton Books 2021

ISBN 978-1-63710-306-7 (paperback)
ISBN 978-1-63710-308-1 (hardcover)
ISBN 978-1-63710-307-4 (digital)

Printed in the United States of America

In loving memory of my father,
Dr. C. P. Ananthasivan, and in dedication
to my mother, Vasantha Ananthasivan, sister Sandhya
Giridhar, and to my Thiruvarpu and Perumbavoor families
who have loved, supported, and encouraged
me in so many immeasurable ways.

CONTENTS

LEADERSHIP PERSPECTIVES

Managers Seeking to Evolve and Lead with Purpose

Instinctively, managers who wish to advance throughout their careers know that they must have impact on business performance; however, they may not have a clear understating of ways to achieve that goal. Sundar Ananthasivan's book provides clear guidance to help managers succeed as they advance from their earliest position to broader leadership responsibilities in more senior roles. Unlike other books focused on general leadership styles and approaches, this book uniquely presents recommendations from Sundar's own experiences, including explicit guidance for each stage of one's career. These recommendations provide a detailed framework to help managers extend their skills to both elevate their impact in their current roles and to prepare for future challenges at their next level of responsibilities. All the recommendations are presented in a very personal style, organized to provide valuable guidance for each of four-defined stages of career development that flow smoothly from initial responsibilities to visionary senior leader. I feel that this book can be a valuable source of guidance throughout a manager's entire career.

—-Dr Thomas Hustad,
Professor Emeritus of Marketing
Kelley School of Business
Indiana University
Bloomington, IN 47405

The thing I remember the most from our conversations was your focus on the intangibles of management and leadership. Too many seminars, self-help books, business coaches, etc. emphasize daily organization, thinking big, leveraging apps and tools, and the list goes on and on. Your approach focuses on the all too often dismissed aspects of impactful managers and leaders—their heart skills. However, a business leader's heart will struggle to flourish in a role that does not align with their purpose. It was an aha moment for me to put those two together. It seems so simple, yet rarely discussed in business leadership.

After collaborating on your conference presentation, I dove into serious self-reflection. I have been stuck on a leadership rung, and the leap to the next seemed daunting. You gave me the gift of a clear step-by-step process to apply, and from it, I gained the insight and clarity I needed to start my journey to a visionary leader. The process was tremendously fulfilling; it felt like I was *grabbing lightning for leadership!*

It's now time for me to put into practice the guidance you elegantly share and move to elevate my impact and engagement levels. The best part? I'm reinvigorated to professional growth again!

Thank you for sharing your wisdom. I believe this book will be an influential guide for many managers and leaders.

Patti Schutte
CEO/Founder and Principal Coach
Be Brilliant Presentation Group

PROLOGUE

As I was traveling back some time ago on a long-haul flight from Asia back to the United States, I was thinking about the year that was and the accomplishments of the team and key leaders. As with any global leader over the last couple of decades, *improve value stream and business KPIs, drive process efficiencies, improve margins, enable revenue growth, increase new products launched and vitality index*, and *implement innovation drivers* were all the key phrases that leaders and teams were used to hearing. These were all part of the typical corporate enablers as a part of the language that was used by or in senior management in policy and strategy deployment meetings in most large corporations today.

One of the young managers who was on my team had asked me, "Sundar, am I growing as a leader? You keep mentioning that I am doing very well with my metrics and goals and that I need to engage more and make a larger impact to grow. How should I think of the impact you talk about? Am I growing?" That was a very fair question. I have been asked similar questions from others during my formal and informal mentorship of younger leaders over the last many years. While many corporations have tools and structures to track metrics and KPIs and even rate behavior of associates, there was not much for an individual to assess his or her own growth path and communicate and assess accordingly with his or her mentor or manager.

Something was missing. All the above-mentioned enablers were typical enterprise drivers of profits and efficiencies, which is essential given the nature of a corporation. All this was pure corporate managerialism. None of these enablers, though, reflected the essence of how an individual felt in terms of a meaningful, purposeful impact in their leadership journey besides achieving or just being in the process of achieving certain business targets. Why was there no measure of how an associate may be evolving in his or her leadership journey? Why was there no pathway to indicate how the leadership KPI of the individual may be evolving? Should be there be such a measure? Could there be such measures?

As I reflected on the question, I realized from my own career leadership evolution that there was a subtle expectation of associates who were leaders, aspiring leaders, or even well into their leadership journey in their careers to figure out the different aspects of leadership and evolve accordingly. But what were these aspects? How does one go about understanding them? Is it from a mentor? Is it from the policy handbook? Is it from general periodic conversations with key people in the organization and outside? If so, what is the basis for those leadership evolution conversations for an aspiring, driven associate? What is a potential path that an individual can rate themselves on in their journey?

Having had the opportunity to work in four different industries and evolve as a leader, my own experiences and journey helped me reflect on the leadership evolution aspects that most people in any corporation typically look for in upcoming and existing leaders. These are typically great skills in a particular subject area, great attitude, curiosity in learning, and a continuous sense of an increase in one's competencies and impact across the organization.

As I continued this reflection, it led me to think of all my career and leadership experiences. There were some companies that were heavily process oriented, and the empathy aspects of relating to people seemed lacking. But these companies absolutely drove for and achieved results through very diligent process rigor. It did not mean there existed no empathy. It only meant that given the drive for results, empathy appeared to take a back seat. In terms of the capital construct, these types of companies managed to achieve most of the results from the initiatives chosen many a time. There were other companies that were less process oriented and achieved a lesser level of success but appeared more empathetic.

At the end of the day, as a leader in any level in the organization, it is about being able to relate to the people. Processes are a way of organizing tasks and workflow, and KPIs are a way of measuring them to see if the workflow is headed in the right direction.

A leader who is purposeful and who can relate to his or her team engenders trust, and this in turn translates to increased efficiency in the processes.

Based on my experiences in different industries and seeing the interplay of processes, cultures, and aspiring leaders and existing leaders, this book is intended as a self-reflection, tracker, and evolution tool for anyone on their leadership journey. It attempts to breakdown the leadership stages into four quadrants with steps and actions to evolve at each stage. I would imagine there are many aspiring leaders or established leaders seeking for ways to assess their leadership stage and potential evolution approaches in their organizations.

I hope that this book allows for some folks to explicitly understand that no process or KPI or even mission and vision definitions can allow for true trust and engagement amongst a group of people, be it in a corporation, a team sport, or a group dance event. True leadership is much about being a glue to a team allowing everyone on the team to thrive with ideas toward achieving a common purpose. The single focus of a leader through a cause (business mission or otherwise) is to be of service to his or her team. Only this can truly allow for derivatives of strategy (KPIs and otherwise) a chance to truly be enabled holistically and meaningfully.

While you may engage in a particular style of leadership given where you are in your career or in life, remember, "it is not where you sit that matters, it is where you stand on how you influence issues that make a difference." As a leader, you can and should always aim to be empathetic and understanding of your team members' strengths and enable them in positions that will help drive and evolve processes. This allows for the human spirit to be fulfilled and unleashes each person's skills and potential to be elevated in a process which in turn will drive business metrics and innovative approaches automatically.

I hope you find the book and its approach meaningful in your leadership journey. If I have managed to share my experiences in the written format, this book should help you assess your current state of leadership and help provoke some thoughts for your next stage of leadership. If that happens for you, then my experiences and this sharing through this book would be so much more meaningful for me. Chapters 1 through 4 talk of leadership elements and the 5P (purpose, people, process, product, portability) approach while chapters 5 through 10 talk about each stage of leadership in a typical corporation you are probably in. Chapter 11 wraps it all up. Chapter 1 is a must read to understand the leadership quotient matrix and where you potentially fit in. You can then move onto the chapter that reflects your position on the leadership quadrant from your assessment. You can then come back to the leadership elements the chapter references for you to pay attention to. Or you can read the whole book from start to finish as you find the time.

The absolute best to you in finding your true purpose, making a positive impact for yourself, your team, your business, the industry you are in, and the society you influence through your actions, products, and services!

I would like to thank all the people I worked with over the years for various learnings and experiences that have shaped my journey. I would especially like to thank Patti Schutte, who further inspired me with some thoughts and ideas as I was writing this book.

CHAPTER 1

The Leadership Premise

Be true to yourself.

—Coach John Wooden

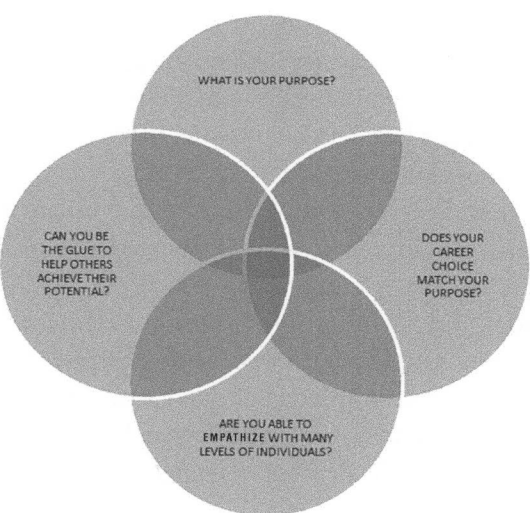

Everyone is intrinsically a leader at some level in their daily lives. There is some focus on family, finances, relationships, health, all of which involve elements of people and processes. This fundamentally suggests that everyone is somewhat structured and disciplined in following some processes to get to somewhere one must be. This also indicates that everyone is already somewhat trained in elements of task management to get somewhere or get something done. After all, every day, everyone must get up, brush one's teeth, shower, make eating choices, take care of family, help their friends and loved ones, keep their minds and body healthy, and through all this work at something that is their passion. This passion, when it matches their purpose with work, allows for a wonderful equilibrium, which then allows for great leadership. What is it then that elevates this individual task management capability—that many of us have at home and in our personal lives and allows us to exist as useful individuals—into leadership in a team environment at work that people will want to hear and act on to achieve a higher common work purpose?

I believe it all starts with, "Are you true to yourself?" If you are reading this book, I am sure you are aware of many of the wonderful folks who are recognized as true or great leaders for their approaches in various team activities, work or sport. John Wooden is one who is well-known and respected for his coaching and mentorship. I believe those two elements are also very critical leadership elements in work as well as sport. His Woodenisms[1] are well-known, but the fundamental essence of his leadership style was that he was true to who he was and what he believed in.

So does that mean anyone who is true to who one is and believes in coaching and mentorship can be a respected and successful leader? Well, those are two key elements that one needs to have as a basis to be a great leader. But there is another very key element as well. Coach John Wooden had one of what I believe is the most important aspect of leadership that was completely aligned with him in being true to himself: faith. I fundamentally believe that faith is the key element that transforms a good leader into a respected, loved, and successful leader. Faith is the glue that links the two elements of coaching and mentorship and allows them to shine through in highlighting the potential of people and bringing them together for a higher common purpose.

By faith here, I am not suggesting religion or a belief in a god but an intrinsic belief in the universe and humanity and having a purpose in making things better. I am referring to the innate desire to be useful to do good with the learnings and experiences one has acquired to allow for the benefit of the larger universe one wants to make an impact in—work or sports or any other effort. I do fundamentally believe that this one aspect is critical to a genuine acceptance of one's ideas in a leadership position by a larger audience which then translates to truly meaningful and successful leadership helping drive a common purpose.

Think of the four questions in the circle above as it applies in a typical large business environment today. These days, whether one is a functionally called an associate, supervisor, manager, director, or senior leader, one has access to many if not all the same tools, i.e., emails, smartphones, projectors, PowerPoint decks, Excel spreadsheets, project plan creation tools, and many more. Why then are many managers and leaders still unable to meaningfully connect their message or purpose to many folks in the business environment? Why do many associates or supervisors feel they should be in higher positions to achieve their purpose or make an impact? After all, one is expected to perform some calculations or track some sales numbers or convey or understand revenue growth numbers, implement some elements standardization procedures, set some performance goals, achieve some major project deadlines, implement elements of technology, develop elements of customer satisfaction and related, right? These are the typical elements of jobs in many businesses over the last few years, right? In today's day and age, with all the trainings, standardization of metrics and procedures, simple funnel diagrams to show new product and service launches, all managers and supervisors should be great leaders, at least in their realms, right? It feels so, in today's value-stream-driven, task, and efficiency-based organizations. If all managers or leaders do this, why are still some more successful than others?

I passionately believe the answer starts with the statement of John Wooden above, "Be true to yourself." All living creatures are possessing intelligence. In human beings, we have been able to identify and differentiate and even somewhat quantify emotional and logical intelligence. When you present the metrics or technology or customer satisfaction message through any of the mechanisms above, all associates and leaders around you can very quickly pick up on how much you truly believe in it or if you are just espousing a set of data/message metrics through the set of corporate business tools. People understand and can relate through their logical and emotional intelligence. If you truly do not have faith in the numbers, messages, and data you are presenting through these tools, all people around you can definitely pick up on the true meaningful value of the message you are trying to communicate. If there is any sense from the team that you are only presenting data or a message (stretch or realistic) with no personal faith that it is toward something meaningful (whatever it may be, business growth, new products, new processes, customer satisfaction, etc.), your leadership quotient (perceived and real), which is a reflection of the purpose and experience stage of your career, will tend to fall in the lower left quadrant of the matrix shown below.

What Is the Leadership Quotient Matrix Value?

The leadership quotient matrix (LQM) is the essence of this book, which aims to help evaluate a leader's evolution based on helping provide an awareness of where a leader is in their career in an organization. It is the basis of the book and aims to quantify leadership evolution in quadrants through highlighting leadership phases, organization perceptions, and self-reflection needs of anyone in a leadership position. The LQM is an attempt at helping associates and leaders at various stages of their career in their thought process to help transition from one leadership phase to another. It is the crux of this book and is intended to help the reader understand the potential leadership journey and the point at which they may be at in their career. This approach should also enable organizations to help evaluate their associates and leaders and help provide the managers and high potentials an evolutionary approach toward sharpening their leadership skills to ultimately achieve their purpose by fueling their passion.

The LQM matrix is an elementary assessment method of quantifying a leader's engagement level in an organization or team with the impact level. At every stage of leadership in an organization, be it a new team lead or supervisor or a growing midmanager or a senior business leader or a visionary, there is an engagement level based on tools and messaging and an impact level that the leader achieves through that engagement.

This matrix attempts to help self-evaluate an associate's understanding of their leadership perspective as well as help the organization with another approach to help assess a leader at any level their engagement and impact. This is immensely powerful as it should help increase the connection in a very tangible manner to engagement and impact (results), I have mentioned in previous pages. It is precisely this connectedness of a person's purpose with his or her team and messaging that with the business or organization's mission that helps tie the impact and engagement levels as a leader more effectively with KPIs and processes, which are the tools to act on purpose.

To take it a step further, your faith in these numbers (KPIs) and or messages that describe or quantify an initiative or stage of an initiative can only come from a deeper faith in your purpose, which comes from a deeper belief in what you want to achieve as a leader. This, in turn, comes from "Are you true to yourself?" If you are truly in a field you want to be and want to enable a change in the arena/industry you are working in, your deep faith, your commitment to your belief (in a product or a cause), and your faithful presentation of the details and commitment to the initiative will all come together. When an intent is included in your messaging with faith, the team will then not only hear your message through the initiatives but feel your faith(intent) and your trueness to the cause, and in turn your being true to yourself in your chosen field and cause.

The LQM can be thought of as a Leadership value matrix that you provide to your area of influence. While it is exceedingly difficult to quantify leadership value as a number or word, it could be broadly thought of in terms of the following:

Leadership value = impact x engagement

While impact and engagement cannot be easily measured by an initiative or a dollar value or number of meetings, it is a concept that allows one to think of how much impact is one having across the organization with a certain level of engagement. The impact could be in terms of success of initiatives, new technology revenue given your engagement in leading it, hiring of talent to evolve your area and the business, cross-functional mentorship, and eventually industry champion. Engagement would be in terms of actions one is working within a subteam, team, or at a senior leadership level and would be in terms of levels of influence within and across the organization that one is having.

The Leadership Quotient Matrix

Impact Level

Enabler Leader

- One-over-one meetings
- Senior leader town hall meetings
- Strategy Senior level meetings
- Coaching, mentoring

Visionary Leader

- Values
- Faith
- Purpose/societal value
- Industry impact
- Teaching/sharing
- Experience sharing

Initial Stage Leader

- PowerPoints
- Metrics
- Process spreadsheets
- Daily management
- One-way boss speaks

Doer or Follow-Only Leader

- Performance management
- Half-Yearly Reviews
- Process metrics based
- Manage time and some aspects of projects or products

Engagement Basis

18

I think it is a question of having a purpose and explaining the commonality of purpose in the business and explaining the various processes and metrics as being tied to that purpose. It sounds simple, but I think many people either miss the purpose part and focus only on the process or metrics or focus on the purpose part but miss on defining trackability through process and products and related. A practical way of looking at it is through the LQM, the leadership quotient matrix. Are you as a leader able to serve your purpose in the quadrant you are in while aiming to grow to the top right quadrant?

Are you as a leader able to articulate the meaning of what the team is doing in terms of the measures applicable to each quadrant and tie it to the larger common purpose which should match your personal purpose?

Do you recognize the quadrant you are in?

Do you think others in your organization would identify you on the same quadrant as you have identified yourself?

In the next few chapters, we will identify the aspects of each quadrant and the approaches to closing the gap as you seek to move from one quadrant to another in evolving your leadership on an impact and engagement basis.

Chapter 1 Thought Points: Leadership Premise

- Do you have the right purpose identified for yourself?
- Is your purpose and passion aligned?
- Do you understand how it relates to the work you are involved in currently?
- Do you understand the impact you are currently making?
- Do you understand your engagement levels in the organization?
- Do you feel you are in the right quadrant based on your impact and engagement levels?
- What would you do differently to impact your LQM value in the organization?

CHAPTER 2

Self-Awareness and Reflection

The dictionary definition of *self-awareness* is "a conscious knowledge of one's own character, feelings, motives, and desires." It is a key element to emotional intelligence (Daniel Goleman), which is a fundamental aspect of any leadership endeavor. Typically, becoming a good listener can increase self-awareness. By being open to others, it allows an individual to listen objectively and process judgments, evaluations, and logical conclusions in an effective manner.

Why is this important here?

To understand your current level of leadership and reflect on where you are in the LQM, one needs to have the knowledge of one's character, feelings, and processing patterns of conclusions. Only if one has some ability to do that can one evolve in their leadership effort since much of leadership is relating to people and moving forward for a common purpose.

How does one become more self-aware as one goes through life and in this case their career in terms of the LQM (developgoodhabits.com, 2020)?

1) Evaluate yourself objectively.
    a. Understand your current perceptions. Think of the items you are good at and that you may need to improve upon. This is about you and not a comparison exercise.
    b. Think of your accomplishments.
    c. Think of your happy moments since childhood.
    d. Obtain honest feedback about yourself from people.

2) Write down your thoughts.
   a. Think about how you are as a leader and how people under you are likely to view you.
   b. Reflect on what you do to help people and how that ties to your values.
   c. If you could do more to help your team, how would you do that? What would that be?
3) Write down your goals and priorities.
   a. Writing down goals helps turn ideas into action steps. Break down these goals into mini goals so that it will not be so overwhelming.
   b. Make sure that these goals are related to three main areas:
      i. Customer related
      ii. Employee related
      iii. Performance related
   c. Identify process goals
   d. Identify outcome goals
   e. Identify strategic long-term goals
   f. Identify tactical short-term goals
   g. Identify the tie-off between all the above and seek alignment in actions and thoughts to be successful.
4) Perform daily self-reflection.
5) Practice meditation and mindfulness.
   a. Meditation is a practice of improving awareness. While there are many types of meditations, the one I am referring to is in terms of self-reflection toward the following:
      i. Your goals.
      ii. What is working and what is not.
      iii. How are you self-limiting, if at all?
      iv. Can you change your processes and improve them?
6) Take personality tests.
   a. Work with your HR team to understand your traits.
   b. HR teams are always willing to help you take Myers-Briggs and other tests to help understand your traits.

7) Ask your friends to describe you.
   a. This will help you reflect and close the gap between your own perception and reality in the eyes of your close friends.
8) Ask for feedback at work.
   a. This can be done in many ways formally and informally. There are elements like a 360 feedback, which can help formally. There are informal elements of seeking feedback in meetings and in general.

All the above eight steps should help you start understanding your own feelings, actions, and judgments and its impact on others and yourself. Once you understand this self-awareness habit, it should help you reflect on your leadership actions and in turn their impact. This should also allow you to take the first steps toward understanding the true quadrant you belong to in your leadership journey.

As we go forward, we will delve into the leadership elements in each quadrant, which should allow for further self-reflection. We will then examine some of the steps and actions that can be taken to close the gaps that will allow for functioning as a visionary leader in the top right quadrant.

Chapter 2 Thought Points: Self-Reflection and Awareness

- Do you understand your purpose?
- Do you understand your reality and how you are perceived by others?
- Have you sought direct feedback?
- Have you sought indirect feedback?
- Have you created a plan?
- Have you begun the quest for self-understanding through reflection or meditation?
- What is your most significant work achievement for the week?

22

CHAPTER 3

The 5P Approach

That leads me to define an approach that has served me well in engaging with teams at many levels. I refer to this approach as the 5P approach. This is people, purpose, process, product, portability. The evolution of this approach for me was in three stages.

Early in my career, this approach started off as a 3P approach, which matured into a 5P approach as I grew in my own understanding through leading teams around the globe, sharing experiences, and serving my purpose.

1. At the early stages of my leadership experiences, as I would examine the right approach for the team in question, I would formulate the question, "Does this organization or team or effort have the right *people* in the right *process* delivering the right *products*?"
2. As my experiences grew and the business world grew increasingly global, I expanded the question to be, "Does this organization have the right *people* in the right *process* delivering the right *products* and is it *portable*?"
3. As I matured in my own personal and leadership growth and understood better the interplay of task management, goal management, enterprise results, and metrics communication, *purpose* became the key element of this leadership approach. It showed itself as the key element of any leadership effort in combination with other elements. This then evolved the question to be, "Does this organization

have the right *people* in the right *process* delivering the right *products* through a *portable* approach starting with the right common *purpose*?"

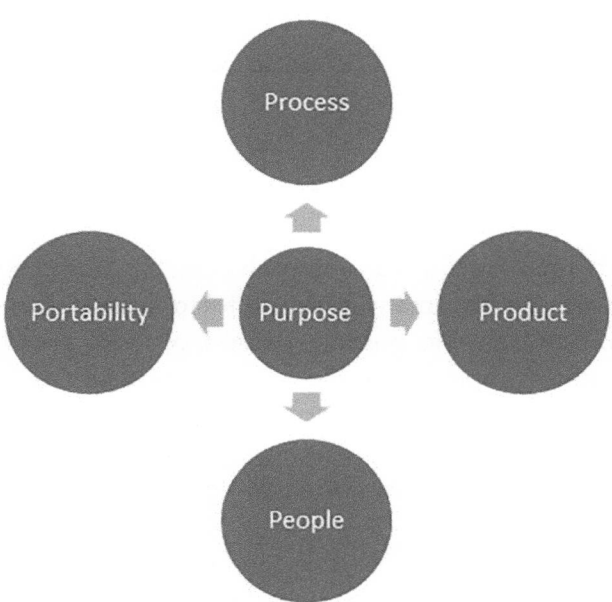

This very element of purpose is what defines a great leader from a good leader (Jim Collins, *Good to Great*). Collins defines a great leader as someone with great professional will and personal humility. I believe the personal humility comes from purpose, a deep desire to subjugate one's ego in the interest of a larger good (purpose). The same element of leadership was illustrated by Coach John Wooden. In the words of Dick Enberg (*Success* magazine, December 2016), a longtime friend of Wooden, "Coach did not impose his religion, his philosophy, his lifestyle on others. He allowed each of us to be an individual. A lot of strong personalities feel that to really fulfill the leadership role, they must change everyone around them and make them like themselves. But Coach wasn't like that." I agree with that. It is all about allowing everyone around you to be their best while serving a common purpose. If the elements of 5P align in the organization that you are in, your leadership journey will evolve and have the right impact at each phase of your journey through the right engagement levels with your purpose partners.

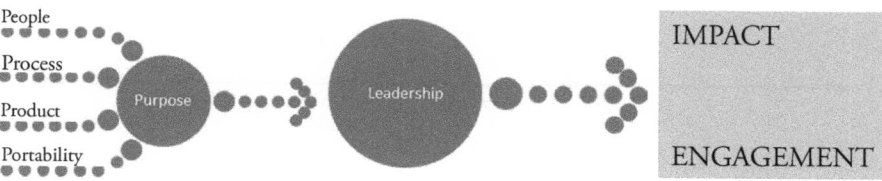

As we go through this journey of exploring the 5Ps, we will look at the various elements, potential tool sets, and skills that contribute to getting to the top right visionary quadrant, the ultimate level of leadership of the LQM where purpose and action on purpose is critical.

Chapter Thought Points: Purpose Defines Leadership

- Do you have the right purpose identified for yourself?
- Is your purpose and passion aligned?
- Do you understand how it relates to the work you are involved in currently?
- Can you see beyond yourself and the ability of others?
- Are you willing to design processes around the strengths of the people with you?
- Are you willing to recognize people are different culturally and come from their own unique experiences?
- Do you realize it is purpose that enables all this to come together for the team's or business or initiative's success?

CHAPTER 4

Empowerment

> As we look into the next century, leaders
> will be those who empower others.

—Bill Gates

Operational Effectiveness—Margin Protectors; - - - Innovation inhibitors Process efficiency builders	People potential enablers—Breakthrough innovators - Industry and society thinkers

Initial Stage Leader—KPI keeper	'Doer Leader' Corporate rule enforcer	Enabler Leader—Corporate Rule Creator	Visionary Leader—Purpose and Humility Based forward thinker

Empowerment is a unique concept in that many leaders are afraid that empowering their teams will result in their loss of power. In fact, it is just the opposite. Empowerment is one of the most powerful enablers for unlocking human potential.

The differences between a manager and a leader have been well documented. Many leaders especially in the manufacturing/design space many a time operate under the nuance that control is critical to the success of an organization. They confuse control for operating mechanisms and process structure and miss empowering the associates to thrive in a correct structure. Allowing the individual to thrive in the correct process structure is one of the keys to impactful team leadership.

At the very essence, empowerment is the function of one's trust and confidence in their purpose. As mentioned earlier, purpose is the key to success in any role especially a leadership role in an organization.

What is the definition of *empowerment?* The business dictionary defines *empowerment* as "a management practice of sharing information, rewards, and power with employees so that they can take initiative and make decisions to solve problems and improve service and performance." Empowerment is based on the idea that giving employees skills, resources, authority, opportunity, motivation, as well as holding them responsible and accountable for outcomes of their actions, will contribute to their competence satisfaction and potential fulfillment.

In order for empowerment to truly occur, one should have the mindset and mentality of a visionary leader, i.e., purpose and humility based. Leaders typically could be in a state of their own evolution in one of the above 4 categories indicated above as they go through their leadership evolution. Getting to the spot of a visionary leader mindset is an evolution which allows for enabling empowerment through the organization. Only if one has the mindset of a visionary leader can one enable a trusting team and empower this team to achieve success in the vision intended for the organization.

What does empowerment look like daily?

A vision is typically achieved through a set of common initiatives. These initiatives are to be clearly defined as a series of strategic planning steps for the team to succeed. These initiatives must be agreed upon by the larger team as the steps toward achieving organizational success.

Once the initiatives for the team have been established for the group or organization you are leading, the next step is to enable milestones (breadcrumbs) for the group to ensure everyone is on the same path. Milestones or KPIs if rightly used and enabled serve as bread-crumbs toward the road to achieve the vision that has been set.

Typically, these breadcrumbs to solve the initiatives toward delivering the vision are in terms of delivery, quality, satisfaction, and cost measures. I have referenced these measures as, typically, any product or service organization has elements of these measures that define its success toward the vision set. These measures will enable the team to stay on the path of making the initiatives successful toward achieving the vision.

Here is where empowerment applies.

If you are early in your career and have typical societal titles of team leader or manager, your main role may be in terms of help-ing track these metrics or breadcrumbs toward achieving the busi-ness initiatives. This is where a leader at this level can utilize this opportunity to understand vision setting and breaking it down into metrics. Organizations need measures to understand direction and a leader can differentiate oneself by not looking at the role as just a job but to understand and help fine-tune the metrics. This will enable the leader in this type of role to expand his or her horizons toward enabling visions and then setting vision later in their career.

In terms of empowerment, one should allow a leader in this position to manage the metrics through their own methods, data col-lection techniques, and definition of submetrics. Leaders here should be allowed to make financial decisions up to certain levels to enable them to be accountable and take responsibility for driving toward this initiative. Some leaders at higher levels fail because they tend to micromanage associate leaders at this level, thereby eroding trust and not enabling development of future leaders.

A leader who is, say, at a manager level is probably in the lower right quadrant in his or her growth path in the organization. If this leader is managing, say, a team leader who is in quadrant 1 of his or her growth, it is the role of the leader in the second quadrant to empower the leader in the first quadrant to help enable the right metrics.

For example, in a typical engineering organization, there may be a team leader who is responsible for a set of design projects that run through the group. This group maybe a team of five or six individuals who are responsible for delivering designs on projects that flow through the larger team.

The measures for this team maybe the classic measures that are applicable for any value stream team in a typical design-manufacturing organization. This would be elements of cost (budget for the team—salaries, over time, supplies), delivery (output of the team, designs to be done within a certain time), quality (get the right outputs correctly the first time), and customer satisfaction (service in terms of all the above three elements for various internal and external customers).

A practical application of empowerment here would be that the manager works in gathering input from the team leader to assess and understand the right measures and processes that would be meaningful for this value stream team to deliver the needed outputs toward the larger team and in turn business goals.

Many managers just impose a set of metrics and do not engage in working with the team leader in advancing or evolving the metrics or processes. This can happen all along the business workflows which then causes the entire team to be mis aligned with the main purpose.

Chapter Thought Points: Empowerment Enables Trust and Thereby Vision Success

- Do you understand the initiatives in your area?
- Have you set the right initiatives and is there team buy-in?
- Are you comfortable letting your team manage their areas of delivery, cost, and quality?
- Does your team clearly understand the above measures as it applies towards their functional area?
- Have you enabled a common tracking system to help understand direction at any point while driving towards the vision?
- Do you empower people on your team to make decisions as applicable to their area and level of responsibility?

CHAPTER 5

Early-Stage Leader
Quadrant 1

Initial Stage Leader

As you are reading this, you may be either a new team leader or manager, a manager who has been doing the job for a few years, or a midlevel manager who is possibly wanting to grow into the next step of your career. The next step in your career will be clearly decided by your engagement basis and the impact level you want for yourself and the team you lead or want to lead as you look ahead in your career.

If you are a relatively newly appointed team leader or manager, you are probably expected to keep projects on schedule, manage expenses within your limited authority limits, keep quality high, and deliver weekly or monthly reports. If you are working in the engineering, design, or manufacturing functions, you are typically managing a certain set of projects or product lines and you lead a team of maybe two to eight people. You manager expects you to keep projects going, deliver defined quality, and have products manufactured and shipped on time to the customer.

If you are in the working in the sales, marketing, or digital fields, you are expected to do the same, except your product is managing relationships and enabling orders. You are expected to grow sales in your region, develop brochures for services and products in your region, enable your website for sufficient web traffic, and achieve hit rate targets. Your manager sets targets for hit rates and customer relationships, and through various measures that you help track, you are enabling broader business goals that are set by senior management. These are typically defined by organizational and in turn functional KPIs or metrics to drive focus in the team by your manager.

As an early-stage leader, you execute using one of these options:

a) You are happy to have a job, and you just tell your team what to do and keep driving for various metrics, goals, and KPIs that your manager has set.

b) You think through these metrics, goals, and KPIs and work with your team by setting actions in a structured manner to help drive business goals.

If you are just happy to have a job and comfortable having the title of team leader or manager, you choose to drive KPIs for your manager through emails, trackers, and enforcing actions at your team.

On the other hand, if you are a committed, passionate, and purposeful individual, you probably chose option b to help match your leadership purpose and passion to meaningfully drive results for the team you lead. In this case, your education, experiences thus far, and drive to make an impact in the areas you want to, skills, and the industry and firm you are with all come together to enable your success on this purposeful journey.

Your choice of a or b is very clearly going to set you on the course for the type of leader you will eventually become or not become! It will also dictate the amount of influence you have in your efforts as a leader in enabling initiatives at your level currently and later in your career as well. At the end of the day, the most successful people are the ones whose passion for doing something matches their life's purpose and the symphony of these two extremely critical elements of leadership coming together causes them to rise to the highest levels in their field and their leadership style.

Let's examine the KPI keeper or initial stage leadership style and influence. This type of person in a company is typically someone who has recently been promoted to a team leader or manager. This person has earned this in the eyes of the corporation either because they have been categorized as a high potential or they have had a few years of service and the organization feels they have outgrown their pay grade or this individual asked to be promoted and managed to convince their higher up for the next role.

In each of the cases, this person is new and is encouraged given this new role. Typically, this involves managing a few more people and being accountable for the following:

a) output of a new team for the individual—delivery, cost, and timeliness;
b) potential midyear and year end reviews; and
c) vacation approvals, and possibly a
d) small expense account.

Whether this role is called a team leader or a manager, the person performing this role has a few direct reports, usually three to ten, and is expected to keep a section of this value stream going. A value stream is typically a set of tasks as it pertains to a given functional area that result in keeping the flow of business going in the area by enabling the work to flow through the organization and revenue be recognized for the business.

If this role is a market manager or market segment team leader, the expectation for this role is to drive a certain dollar value of products or services into the market against an established target. The group of people reporting to this person have a set of territories and typically need to perform a set of tasks in to achieve the marketing function overall goals.

If this role is that of a design manager in the design value stream, the expectation is to drive a certain number of drawings or designs per a predefined on-time metric and with a certain predefined quality metric to help deliver the product or service the market manager in the other value stream has committed to the customer per business commitments.

If this role is that of an operations team leader or manager, the expectation is typically to establish the production of the product to be delivered in terms of the shift, people involved, and machines to match the same predefined on time and high-quality delivery per business commitments.

Irrespective of the value stream where the job needs to be done, the typical expectation in this role is to do the following:

A) Track the data
B) Report the data
C) Answer emails pertaining to data
D) Speed up things for the customer
E) Extoll the value streams to enhance their speed and quality and possibly
F) Monitor the people on the team for performance to achieve the predefined metrics

At this stage of leadership in most organizations, the key element of such a role is margin protector or efficiency maintainer. Refer graphic on Page 26.

Your success in your career and your profession long-term is going to be absolutely be decided on which of the options you choose on Page 31.

If you choose to adopt the leadership style as described in option a, i.e., just follow the KPIs set for you, engage in just boss speak, and not collaborate and motivate your team, you are setting the course for a long term of staying in the same role or type of role at best, i.e., leading a small value stream, forcing your team to do certain things to achieve the results, and keep your job.

On the other hand, if you are driven and truly want to motivate your team for the best possible performance, you engage with the team on the goals and direction you have been provided from your leader, i.e., option b, and not just roll out the metrics and ask them to do it.

What typically happens in option b, which sets a person up for the next level of leadership, are the following:

a) You discuss the goals for the value stream you lead.
b) You discuss the KPIs that have been requested of the team.

c) You discuss elements of the process your team is responsible for.

d) You seek input from the team.

e) You start creating a basic action plan for milestones and timelines.

These set of actions described above create the key element of trust within the team, which will enable a higher morale and, in turn, optimum productivity. These actions will also enable to engender trust from your manager who will see your behavior and actions in a focused light.

This, in turn, will set you up for further opportunities to enhance your leadership skills and allow for the progression of your career. This will allow your team to feel included in the process and feel a sense of empowerment. This is your first major step in empowerment, which is a key aspect of leadership at every stage. The more you allow your team to feel included and empowered in the goal at hand toward a larger purpose, the more definite is your sense of achieving long-term industry and impact making success in your field and in society.

Chapter Thought Points: Building Trust through Engagement and Empowerment versus "Just Do as I say"

- Do you understand the initiatives in your area?
- Do you understand the quantitative and qualitative measurements for your value stream?
- Are you able to communicate the KPIs set for the value stream effectively to your team?
- Are you able to get buy in for the set KPIs from your team without forcing them to do it?
- Are you able to seek input from your team and accept it even if it differs from your original thought?
- Can you create an action plan with the team with key elements of milestones and timelines?

CHAPTER 6

Preparing for the Next Level

Understanding beyond your immediate Value Stream

At the stage of your career, you have probably spent at least a couple of years of leading a small value stream team. You have understood the sequence of driving for KPIs that are set from the top, worked with your small team to understand the KPIs, and enable them through actions, tasks, and action plans. You understand the process tasks in your area and have a good understanding of the tools used to solve problems, create documents, draw process flow maps for your area, and report out your team's performance in some manner.

You may be wondering what it will be that will enable your thought process to flourish and the organization to have a greater visibility to your potential. You may want to do more but are unsure of what the next steps are.

6.1 Preparation

As one comes into their third or fourth year of initial leadership, the transition efforts toward broadening one's influence and elevating to the next level of leadership begins. This transition effort preparation should include all the aspects of transitioning from a just a job or initial stage leader level to a doer leader and an enabler leader.

This will now involve understanding the detailed process elements of the workflow on both sides of the value stream you lead and a larger business understanding. This will also involve having a deeper understanding of the KPIs and measures that you have been asked to maintain given your initial stage of leadership. This translates to evolving to the next stage of margin protector leader, where you now get to have a say in the metrics and add and subtract metrics based on your experiences over the initial years of the workings of the processes you lead or manage. You also need to help gain additional buy-in from the team by highlighting your knowledge and interest in other business aspects besides just your value stream.

This increased understanding of the business could be through formal organizational programs or could be through individual learnings or a combination of both.

What does all that mean?

This means a leader who is seeking to evolve in a corporation or business now must evolve mentally to understand what the aspects of the workflow are that are involved in the previous value stream and the value stream post his or her own value stream. This is now part of connecting to the bigger picture of the business.

How does one do that?

Five levels of competency understanding are key. These competencies for leadership growth are listed below. Each of these competencies need to be evaluated and evolved with the 5P model in mind. As one understands how to relate to the concept of purpose, people, process, product, portability and tie it to the competency growth listed below, one will notice their engagements and influence to be increasingly effective in the organization as they make strides in their leadership evolution as the business evolves.

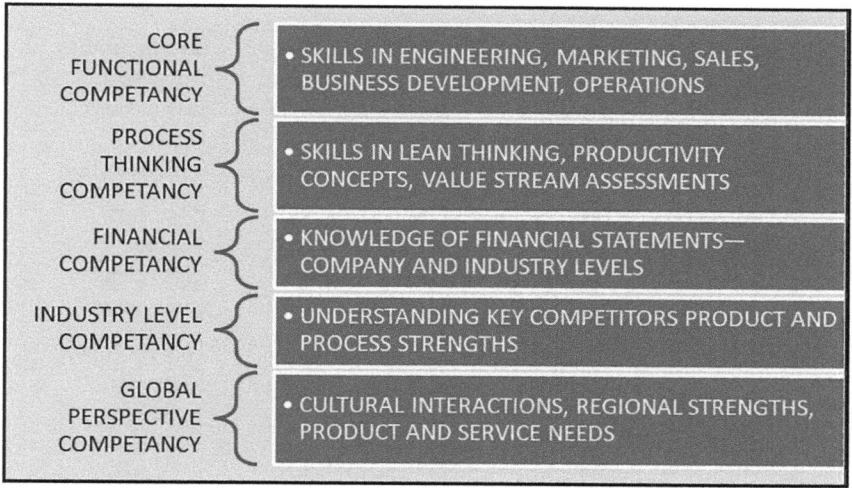

CORE FUNCTIONAL COMPETANCY
• SKILLS IN ENGINEERING, MARKETING, SALES, BUSINESS DEVELOPMENT, OPERATIONS

PROCESS THINKING COMPETANCY
• SKILLS IN LEAN THINKING, PRODUCTIVITY CONCEPTS, VALUE STREAM ASSESSMENTS

FINANCIAL COMPETANCY
• KNOWLEDGE OF FINANCIAL STATEMENTS— COMPANY AND INDUSTRY LEVELS

INDUSTRY LEVEL COMPETANCY
• UNDERSTANDING KEY COMPETITORS PRODUCT AND PROCESS STRENGTHS

GLOBAL PERSPECTIVE COMPETANCY
• CULTURAL INTERACTIONS, REGIONAL STRENGTHS, PRODUCT AND SERVICE NEEDS

These competencies are key in transitioning from just a job or initial stage leader into a doer leader and then onward onto an enabler leader and further into an understanding, result-oriented visionary leader. What does that mean?

Up until this stage of your career, you have executed what has been asked of you. At this point, you will have an exceptionally good understanding of how the KPIs are tracked. From this point onward, your innate understanding of these KPIs and immediate work processes should transition into the deeper aspects of how the KPIs are tied to the above competencies for your growth in a business and business growth itself.

Let us examine what that means.

Core Functional Competency

Table 1. Identifying Core Elements and Interactions (Engineering)

Item	Function (Engineering)	Obligation	Competency
Subject matter	Material strength	Demonstrate analytical abilities	Integrate analytical ability with design strategy
Testing	Hypothesis prove out	Understand and integrate analytical and digital validation	Strong product behavior and performance needs understanding
Standardization	Reuse	Emphasize standard selections for lead time gains where applicable	Platforms, systems, subsystems, components
Design	Form, fit, and function	Message value of each feature of the design	Design, Products, Materials, Technology
NPI	Stage gate	Demonstrate Stage-Gate rigor	Understanding VOC and translating into design feature value

Context: Typical design engineering environment in a firm producing designed products.

The above table highlights some of the key elements of leadership as one transitions to the next stage from a functional excellence perspective in a typical engineering function. The same table and approach can be used to identify core elements of excellence needed in a marketing or operations or supply chain or other business functions.

Some of the key process competencies required of a leader are in table 2.

Table 2: Core Process Elements

Item	Process Elements	Obligation	Competency
Process flow	Workflow, steps, touchpoints, lean	Ensure workflows through the department(s) with the least amount of touches	Understand efficiency concepts
CI	Kaizens, A3s, root cause analysis, fishbone	Enable tools in the department and across	Knowledge of CI tools and cross-functional collaboration
Productivity	Lead times, capacity	Manage optimum capacity to satisfy business lead times commitments	KPI development and management

Context: For typical businesses where processes involve steps, tools, and flow between groups.

Many businesses typically involve processes to move work through the organization. The ability of a leader to optimize the process workflow and gain maximum efficiencies is a critical ability at each stage of the leadership evolution. One of the key elements in understanding process elements is the difference and synergies between effectiveness and efficiency. This is explained in the figure below.

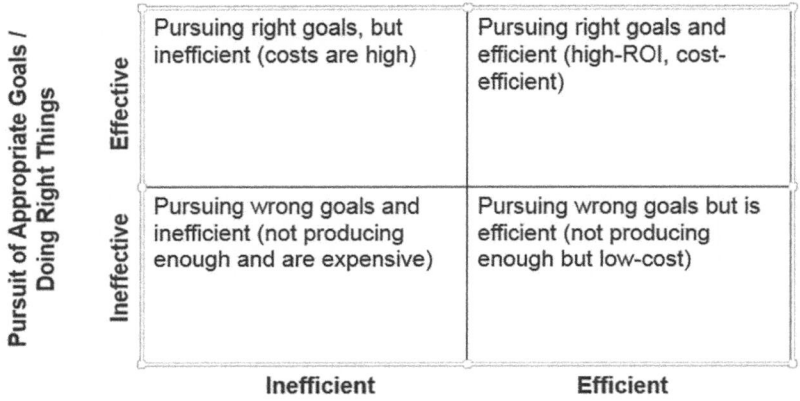

Source: https://www.insightsquared.com

As a leader evolves from one stage to another, a keen knowledge of the financial aspects of the business is very key. Understanding of financials is critical to understanding how KPIs are set and how their interplays affect various aspects of business financial elements. Understanding the managerial aspects initially and capital aspects of finance soon after can help a leader evolve quickly from any function, they may be operating in.

Table 3: Typical Financial Elements

Item	Process Elements	Obligation	Competency
Managerial finance	Budgets, tracking, credits, debits	Allocate and manage budgets	Understand credits and financial tracking systems in the business
Capital finance	Cash flow statements, income statement, and balance sheet	Manage budgets and spending in relation to EBIT and SG&A requirements	Knowledge of financial elements of the statements and its relationship in business

Context: For typical businesses.

Table 4: Industry-Level Elements

Item	Industry Elements	Obligation	Competency
Market landscape	Perfect competition, monopolistic competition, oligopoly, monopoly	Understand what segment of the market	Understand the nature of competition and plan processes accordingly
Competitive benchmarking	Elements of competitor products and services	Demonstrate keen understanding of key competitor products and features	Knowledge of markets, products, services, and features preferred by customers in each geographical area

| New entrants | Understand business model and services | Demonstrate understanding of new entrant price points and customer relationship models | Understand service and product offerings, channel, and delivery models to customers of new entrant |

Context: For typical businesses as in any industry.

Table 5. Global Perspectives Elements

Item	Global Elements	Obligation	Competency
Global presence	Continents, countries, and regions	Demonstrate understanding of business presence	Understand why business has chosen presence in each region
Products	Types of products and performance of each product	Understand each product and reason for being sold in each region	Product performance understanding as linked to regional product needs
Service model	Lead time understanding by region for service levels required	Demonstrate understanding of lead times by function in the business by region	Business elements, i.e., sales timing, quote timing, drawing timing, product delivery timing by service level, and product type

Culture	Norms, business protocols, food habits, timings	Respectful understanding of regional nuances and workings	Soft skills in terms of work and nonwork protocols, meeting etiquette, pre reads, implementation methodologies of software and processes besides clear product needs understanding

Context: Typical global business with locations in majority continents.

The above elements by area outline some of the key elements required for a leader to elevate his or her understanding to the next level for functional and career business success. The understanding of these elements and gains in understanding of these elements will allow the expansion of one's mind to tie together:

a) The reasons for business presence globally
b) The financials associated with revenues in other regions
c) The need for enhancing KPIs in the value stream to serve local functional or larger business needs
d) The need for enhancing processes for increased efficiencies and thereby set the stage for understanding the reasons for various KPIs and processes that have been currently set

Chapter Thought Points: Preparing for the Next Level

- Do you understand the initiatives in your area?
- Do you understand the workflow in your current area of leadership?
- Do you understand the tasks involved in the above workflow?
- Do you recognize key elements of what some of the associates in this workflow do?
- Do you understand the purpose for your business?
- Do you understand the various functional competencies?
- Can you relate your area's performance with respect to other functions?
- Do you understand the need for increasing the width of knowledge through the competencies listed in the tables?
- Do you have formal and informal methods of gaining these competencies?

CHAPTER 7

The Next-Level Elements
Quadrant 2

Midstage Leader

As you are reading this, you are probably a manager who has led a team for a few years and are looking to take the next step of your career. Each next step in your career will be clearly decided by your engagement basis and the impact level you want for yourself and the team you lead or want to lead as you look ahead in your career. This is outlined on page 18 in the LQ matrix.

At this stage, your typical work outlook may include leading a team leader or two and ten to fourteen or so direct reports. You are responsible for creating goals for the team, assign these in a company-mandated goal calibration system, monitor the metrics in your areas, and keep a few key initiatives in your functional area running.

You should be able to perceive that your engagement level with your team is higher than in your earlier years especially in term of self-reflection and awareness and in terms of the following:

a) Goal setting
b) Metrics selection
c) Key initiatives drivers
d) Initial stages of coaching and mentoring your team leaders

e) Identifying associates with high potential in setting them and yourself up for your next leadership evolution

You have most probably reached this level of leadership or higher level of managerial evolution in your business because you had chosen option b on page 31 in your engagement style and approach toward your career. In this approach, you have essentially included the team in enhancing the functioning of your value stream and not just mandated your perspectives. At this stage of your career in the organization, you understand the following:

a) The workflow in your value stream
b) The tasks in this workflow
c) The measures (KPIs) set by the business and you to for the workflow
d) The efficiency and effectiveness of the workflow in terms of capacity, lead times, delivery, and quality,
e) Most importantly, the people-process interplay in this workflow that was described in chapter 3, the 5P approach

At this stage in your career, it is very critical to understand how the people you lead through executing the company vision, initiatives, and metrics are situated in the process in your workflow and the larger business process. The moment you understand this relationship and start seeing the value basis of the interplay of people and process, you are now starting to see and further enable the bigger picture of the following:

a) Business goals
b) Efficiency and effectiveness initiatives
c) Interplay of people and processes in your workflow as well as in your adjacent workflows
d) How all this is tied together for the business

At this stage, you are probably a part of the midlevel group of leaders/managers in your company who are responsible for your value streams. You may also be responsible for some key initiatives that are cross-functional and serve a larger business purpose. For example, you may be a R&D manager working with a sales, supply chain, engineering, and operations manager responsible for launching a new product on time. Or you may be a product manager responsible for carving out a new product management strategy in collaboration with the R and D, engineering, and sales managers.

It is these above initiatives that you have been identified for by other leaders in the business that will enable you to enhance your engagement basis on the lower right of the LQM matrix. This will also allow you to showcase your cross-functional skills, which in turn will increase your engagement basis. Cross-functional projects are always key to enhance engagement basis in any organization at any level. This is a key for you to note at this stage and any stage of your leadership.

At this stage, in the lower right quadrant of the LQM, your role typically involves elements of the following:

a) Performance management
b) Goal setting
c) Driving and delivering on metrics
d) Driving revenue, enabling standards and one to two key initiatives in the workstream you lead
e) Identifying a couple of high potentials in your workstream for the business

If you can lead your team in all these areas and are consistently achieving results, it indicates to you and the business you are in that

a) you understand your workflow,
b) you understand the people-process interplay,
c) you understand the role of metrics and can work toward quantifying them meaningfully and qualitatively drive them for the business,
d) you are capable of delivering on performance parameters set and that you have committed to achieve, and

e) you recognize the strengths of all people on your team and can identify high potential associates on the team for future growth

At this stage your engagement and impact level on the business should be at an increasing level. This should be reflected in the following:

a) Your own personal fulfillment
b) Your organization's recognition of your efforts at your level
c) Your team's recognition of your leadership through the engagement and impact you have had on the team and business
d) Your own understanding of people- process interplays

You should now have a sense for how your purpose is being achieved through your leadership with the elements of people-process coming into focus for you more clearly.

All the above should help you reflect clearly in terms of elements of the previous chapter. Table 1 and 2 highlight core functional expertise elements and core process elements. Through these years of leadership as an early-stage leader and now a midstage leader, the elements of your functional strengths and the elements of related processes should come into focus and in your vision much more clearly now.

The core functional expertise of yours in your area whether it is engineering, marketing, operations, or finance should be well established by now and the process elements concepts of workflow, efficiency, effectiveness, and standards should be natural for you at this stage of your leadership evolution.

If it is not self-evident at this stage for you, a reflection and revisiting of chapter 2 is suggested. Self-awareness is a very key leadership ability and reflecting through the points highlighted in that chapter can help you build on this key ability. This will help you assess your midstage leadership impact and engagement levels and prepare you for the next stage.

Chapter Thought Points: Increased Engagement level—Midstage Leader

- Do you understand the initiatives in your area?
- Do you understand the people-process interplay in your workstream?
- Do you understand the workflow tie-offs to your adjacent workflows?
- Do you see synergies in KPIs between your workflows and adjacent workflows?
- Are you comfortable identifying high potential associates in your area?
- Can you see the core functional and process elements in your workstream?
- Do you know which initiatives are key for the business that you are a part of or are leading?
- Are you leveraging those initiatives to build your cross-functional engagement?
- Do you see your leadership quotient (LQ) increasing year over year?
- Is engagement driving your LQ more than impact or both?
- Have you sought feedback on your LQ?
- If so, how does it match your self-awareness and reflection elements?

CHAPTER 8

Enabler Leader Elements

At this stage in your career, you are probably a manager or senior manager who has managed a certain team or teams and are the right bottom quadrant probably in our definitions. You are looking to take your career to the next step and are wondering what the elements of that would be.

You should have developed some aware ness by now of how management is about managing complexity and leadership is about managing change. Most of your efforts thus far have been in the lower two quadrants as you have increased your engagement level with your associates. In the early-stage leader category, you enabled whatever your manager wanted you to and made sure items were done on time.

In your midstage leader experience, you enabled performance reviews, worked with your teams on metrics, and presented key topics to the team. All these efforts were related to your engagement basis. You made an impact on your team and the business but more so in terms of keeping the processes going and enabling the operating margins to be at the levels the business expected them to. You would have maintained and enhanced the KPIs in your workstream and given a sense to the larger business that you understand your workflow tasks and the adjacent area workflow tasks very well. This would have come through in the various meetings that you engaged in daily with your team and other cross-functional teams.

Through this leadership growth and evolution process, if you were following some of the self-awareness guidelines discussed in chapter 2, you would have continuously reflected on your career in terms of feedback, assessment of people, business direction, market headwinds, high potential growth, and strategy interpretation into actionable items for your team.

At this stage in your career as a leader at the midstage and evolving to enabler leader, you would have made strides in your engagement level across the organization, i.e., this would be along the x-axis of the LQM matrix. Your peers in other functions of the business would have seen significant engagement from you on projects and initiatives and your ability to deliver from your team.

Your strengths in your function, be it engineering, operations, IT, or otherwise, would be evident to the organization, and you would have engaged with your peers to enable the work flowing through your portion of the value stream. You would have delivered the KPI targets in your area and your work ethic and approach would be respected by your peers.

The last two stages of your leadership evolution were all about your functional excellence and your process enablement. You would have clearly understood the various functional elements of your role, understood the nuances and the technicalities, and worked with your cross-functional peers on enabling workflows and tying off process needs. Through various process trainings, learning, and engagement on the process elements of table 2 in chapter 6, you would have gained proficiencies on the understanding, use and leveraging of concepts of

A) efficiencies,
B) productivity,
C) CI tools and
D) structured process evaluations using formal tools, like Kaizens, Fishbone diagrams, and related,

to help your team and related cross-functional workflow improvements. You should have seen systemic improvements in the tracking of data, improving on the data and improvement of workflow elements between your area of the value stream and adjacent workflow areas. All these activities and improvements are related to the engagement basis of your leadership.

In order to elevate your leadership to the next level, it is the quadrant 3 elements that are now in focus for you. These include the following:

E) The financial elements competency
F) The industry-level competency
G) The global-level competency

Your skills and knowledge in the financial elements are key for your success in the business you are in. At the end of the day, in a for profit enterprise, all activities in various areas of the business are designed to have success in the top and bottom line. The success of a business depends on how well those activities are tied off together and how well you as a leader of a certain set of those activities in your area enable the workflow through your team with other leaders who manage their areas of the workflow.

The above concept is the first major leadership concept to your elevation as an enabler leader in the organization. It is also the first major concept in increasing your impact on the organization. Thus far, all your leadership actions have been focused on function and process, which are the key elements of the engagement basis. Going forward, it is all about increasing your impact to further your purpose and the ability to inject your style and purpose elements to shape the business for further success.

Financial Competency

In terms of the financial elements, it is key for your larger business success and impact to understand the details of the following:

— Cash flow statement
— Income statement
— The balance sheet

This is extremely critical for your career and leadership growth if you want to grow as a leader in the business and make a larger impact on the business.

You may already be managing an operational expense account for your team's salaries and expenses, a capital expense account for managing your team's spend on new software or small machinery, and a miscellaneous account.

Do you understand clearly how your decisions with these accounts affect the larger business? Do you understand why you have been given these numbers for your budget? Do you understand how your team and tools (software) or hardware have an impact on the business financials?

This is where your knowledge of the above three financial statements becomes critical for your leadership growth. This will not only broaden your career leadership growth but also enable you to understand larger industry and global business financial effects and goings on better. To further your financial competency, you will need to learn through one of these avenues:

a) A training plan provided by your business
b) Self-learn through various online and certificate courses available
c) Engage in formal schooling for certification in financial aspects of a business.

This has to be coordinated with your leader as an individual development plan discussion or in your career path discussion. This will enable you to clearly engage in strategic discussions as your grow in your career given that you have already led and understand clearly the functional and process aspects of your workflow/value stream.

Industry-Level Competency

Industry competency elements are the second of the key elements to evolve your leadership to the next level and reach quadrant

3 of the LQM matrix. This competency involves understanding the different activities and service models as it relates to your business in your industry. In order for you to make an impact at the enabler level of leadership, you will need to start evolving strategy elements in your discussions with your peers and leadership. For this, you will need to understand the following:

a) Key competitors in your industry
b) Their key strengths in terms of products and service models
c) Their market segment and distribution models
d) Their price points
e) Their business structure in terms of elements of vertical integration or otherwise
f) Their forays into the market with newer technologies, like AI, 3D printing, on-demand flexible service models, response times, service levels, existing product models
g) Competitive intelligence on innovation spending for newer services or products
h) Newer acquisitions
i) Potential acquisitions for your business

Focusing on these elements on a continuous basis will help you gain an understanding into your industry at a deeper level. This will enable you to have impactful discussions while you are discussing strategy or involved in strategy implementation meetings in your business.

How do you go about gaining such knowledge?

Some of the ways of going about this are just simply being proactive. Never wait for your business to tell you how to gain this knowledge. Unless you are part of a strategic portfolio management group in a business, this information is not typically or readily available to you. Some of the ways you can keep abreast or even ahead in gaining such knowledge include the following:

a) Subscribe to industry magazines and online webpages
b) Participate in industry forums

c) Attend trade shows
d) Subscribe to financial industry news
e) Attend technology shows in areas pertaining to your industry
f) Pay attention to corporate news from your CEO or board of directors

All the above points should enable you to gain continuous access to information pertaining to your industry and the competition to your business. The financial news relating to your industry should now allow you to compare the key financial metrics of your business to your competitors.

For example, if your business SG&A (selling, general, and administrative) expenses are greater than your competitor of equal size, you should start thinking in terms of what elements of your business are costing you more that your competition is able to achieve at lower costs. If your competition is strongly focusing on AI (artificial intelligence) technologies suddenly and looking at acquisitions in the area or increasing spending on innovation, some questions in your mind should be the following:

- Why are they doing so?
- What will that do for your business?
- What will that do for your business growth or survival?
- What elements of your product development, acquisition or workflow do you need to change to effectively compete with this new threat from your competition?

Global Competency

Today's businesses are very global in nature. Your competition is not the typical statewide or countrywide player. Depending on your industry's penetration ease, competition is always a factor to be considered in annual planning or strategy exercises. Your evolution as a leader and a visionary will depend very much on your ability to leverage the various regulations in your industry and help shape them as the industry evolves. For this, your knowledge of your business and your competitions' presence around the globe in terms of the following:

a) Presence
b) Products
c) Service models

will be key in your evolution as a leader and the impact you make going forward.

While up until this time of your career, your efforts and focus has been on *engagement* (along the x-axis of the LQM), your learnings and evolution through learning in the above areas will be key for your move and success in the third quadrant as an enabler leader. The above learnings and knowledge through your own and business involved efforts will enable you to successfully move to a high *impact* level in the organization, business, and slowly, in the industry.

Chapter Thought Points: Move toward Increased Impact Level—Enabler Leader Thoughts

- Do you understand your engagement efforts thus far in your leadership?
- Would your self-reflection allow you to see what you have achieved in terms of workflow efficiencies and KPI successes thus far at your midstage of your leadership career?
- Do you feel the drive in you for the need to make a larger impact in the business?
- Do you understand your strengths in the functional and process elements thus far?
- Can you tie the above strengths to your fulfillment and business successes since you began your leadership journey?
- Can you tie your workflow and team successes to the business success?
- If your answers to some of the questions above are yes, you are ready to move to the impact stage of your leadership.
- Do you understand where to gain financial, industry, and global competency elements as it relates to your firm?
- Do you have the drive to make a larger impact with the above competency gains?

CHAPTER 9

Enabler Leader Actions

At the stage in your career, as you are reading this, you can probably identify yourself in the organization you work for as a director, senior director, or vice president or a business unit general manager. These are typical organizational titles for leaders intended to make a larger impact and influence a larger portion of the organization.

At this stage in your career, you

- are considered an expert in your functional area;
- have typically led a team of ten or more at least a couple of times in your career thus far, understood the impact of KPIs for your functional area;
- understand various process elements of interface and related tools to improve effectiveness and efficiencies around your value stream and workflow; and
- have gained financial competency in terms of the elements of budget planning, forecasting, understanding of your business performance in terms of income, cash flow, assets, and liabilities and the corporations earnings per share (EPS) at a minimum.

Going forward, your journey toward increased leadership success will be along the lines of the following:

a) Influencing workflows across the organization
b) Increased alignment with other cross-functional business leaders
c) Increased alignment with cross-business-unit leaders in the corporation
d) Increased engagement through the people, process, product, portability approach
e) Direct engagement with key associates who do not report to you but are high potential associates in the organization
f) Strategy planning from a functional perspective for the business
g) Impact on business growth through revenue driver's enablement and technology focus

As you evaluate all the items above, it should become evident to you in each of the seven items listed above, that, they are all related to either the people aspect of the business or influence the process aspect of the business or are tied to the product aspect of the business and are not only local to the business unit you work in but also the larger corporation (portability).

a. Influencing Workflows

As a leader in this position as an enabler leader, you have the luxury and experience to see how the order (contract) that your business receives or service that your business provides is processed by various people using various digital and physical tools in the organization. Through your experience in your prior functional roles, you will be able to see the inefficiencies and waste in the organization. Given this ability and opportunity in your role, you will now need to start influencing the workflow with your peers to enable improved workflows and processes. This is where the process expertise that you have gained earlier in your leadership evolution comes into play at a higher level.

You will have to carve out key initiatives through sponsorship of these by table setting the need and value of these initiatives with your peers. These initiatives are key to changing the trajectory of a particular workflow in the organization that may have been stagnant for a long time and in need of change given changing market dynamics and conditions. Your role in sponsoring and tabling such events for influencing workflows cannot be over stated for the sustainability and growth of the organization.

b. Increased Alignment with Cross-Functional Business Leaders

One of the key leadership elements and qualities is trust. Like in any relationship, this has to be built through constant actions and search for alignment. Leaders at this level are a product of varied experiences out of many different backgrounds. It is very rare that an entire team grows together through the same culture in these days given the dynamics of business, global effects, and local needs. Leaders will have and should have differing ideas on how best to solve a business issue and this is a function of their experiences and education. But alignment in terms of a solution is a must for effective problem solving for the business. At this stage of leadership, decisions and initiatives affect the whole business and not just the function as prior decisions made by you. Hence alignment of an initiative or an approach to solving or fixing an issue becomes extremely critical. If not, teams across the organizational will see the disconnect and business needs and wants will not improve at the rate needed causing slow sustained or quick damage to the business based on the degree of mis alignment.

c. Increased Engagement with Cross-Business-Unit Leaders

At this stage of your leadership, besides influencing your own business unit needs, there will be larger corporation strategy around cross-business-unit efficiencies and effectiveness. Typically, they will be in order to create increased shareholder value for the most optimum leverage of resources within various business units to serve the markets. Toward this, at this stage of your leadership, you will have to engage with your peers and others at other business units to strategize and implement various small and large projects all built around enhancing business tools, business resources, and product utilization across the corporation. This will not only increase synergies between the business units but enable larger goals of standardization, resource utilization, and corporation performance toward the market and its shareholders.

d. Increased People, Process, Product, Portability Engagement

Given that your role now is increasingly about directing workflows and evolving people, processes, and products, perceiving your leadership role through this lens of people, process, product, and portability becomes extremely important. This approach lends itself to systemic enhancements and evolution of the business while other engagements lend themselves to tactical low-level decisions that influence a problem at hand but may not enhance the whole business workflow as needed. This is one of the key changes a leader at this level will have to make to see the business through this broader lens for further growth of the business and self as a leader. This approach is a very structured approach toward evaluating the business and provides a methodical manner for a leader to evaluate the business elements.

e. Increased Engagement with High Potentials

The most important element of a business or any enterprise is the people. Leaders at this level must pay particular attention to key individuals who can contribute to the growth and direction of the company and help shepherd their journeys into leadership. A suggested approach is to have periodic formal and informal engagements with these individuals who typically may not be your direct reports. These individuals have been noticed by you and other leaders in the organization for their drive, skills, engagements, and ability to produce results. These individuals may currently be individual contributors in the organization or maybe team leaders or new managers. The systems and mechanisms in the business may not allow for their visibility directly, but through observations in meetings or other presentations, these individuals will evidence through their work. This act of identifying these individuals formally and informally and helping mentor and coach them in the skills and competencies needed for the future and making pathways for their growth is one of the most important aspects of leadership one can do in this and higher roles.

f. Strategy Planning

All the above elements discussed at this level of leadership come together in the business annual strategy planning sessions. Your ability to articulate, present, enable, and evolve key initiatives needed for the business are critical in your leadership success at this level and the business success. It is the first major step in your having an impact on the organization at large and taking the first steps toward influencing the industry you are in. Your ability to read the market through market data, understand your people through the people and high-potential engagements, shape initiatives to change the course or enhance the course for the business, increase your alignment with your partners in the business, and across the corporation all lead to engagement for the business in terms of strategy with the highest leaders in the business.

Your ability to crystallize these elements as a leader will shape your further success in the business and in the industry.

> **Chapter Thought Points: Move toward Increased Impact Level—Enabler Leader Actions**
> - Do you understand what you need to influence across the organization?
> - How are you identifying these as initiatives and bringing it up to the organization?
> - Are you able to quantify the impact of these initiatives for the organization?
> - Are you able to align these initiatives with your business unit peers?
> - Are you able to align larger initiatives with cross-business-unit peers?
> - Do you have a methodology for identifying and encouraging hi-potentials?
> - Do you understand how all the above influencing and aligning activities help engage your peers on strategy elements?
> - Are you able to see the results of your alignment and initiatives in strategy as business results and people growth?
> - Are you ready and wanting to influence the industry you are in?

CHAPTER 10

Visionary Leader

Most of us go to our graves with our music still inside us, unplayed.

—Oliver Wendell Holmes

To be nobody but yourself in a world which is doing its best, night and day, to make you everybody else, means to fight the hardest battle which any human being can fight; and never stop fighting.

—E. E. Cummings

Visionary: "a person who has the ability to imagine how a country, society, industry, etc. will develop in the future and to plan in a suitable way"

—*Cambridge* dictionary definition

1. Visionary Leader Evolution Elements

At this stage in your career, you have thus far evolved from an

a)   initial stage workflow and metrics manager into
b)   a process efficiency thinker manager into
c)   a high-potential identifier and innovation driver in the business

As you reflect on your journey in the business and industry you are in, the earlier parts of your leadership journey should highlight elements of

a) cost effectiveness initiatives you were part of and led
b) workflow processes you helped evolve and build
c) product defeaturing initiatives that saved costs and increased margins
d) cross-functional and potentially intra business unit processes that added to efficiencies

All the above elements are elements of margin protection or efficiency builders and possibly some growth and innovation drivers as identified in chapter 4. These are key elements that have shaped your corporate and business leadership journey in fine tuning your tools in the areas of efficiencies toward value creation for the business.

As an enabler leader in your most recent evolution portion of your leadership journey, you would have engaged in increased impact-engagement efforts through strategy initiatives creation for the business and high-potential-people engagement. Part of this engagement would also have been in terms of driving innovation for the business you are in. Driving innovation occurs in various areas, and as an enabler leader, you would have driven innovation by strategizing and enabling new services, products, offerings, delivery methods, manufacturing methods, and markets.

Through this, you would have gained exposure and influenced new digital tools, new related technologies, and new financial and project tools for the business and more importantly gained an insight into what the market and key competitors are engaged in.

At this stage, you have all the elements of knowledge, tools, and exposure in your business and the industry to influence your business growth and the industry or industries you have been part of. As listed in chapter 4, the keys to evolving naturally to this form of leadership involves much higher levels of thinking assuming one has the other elements of tools, experience, and knowledge gained in the other areas listed in all the prior chapters.

The next level of leadership involves some deeply personal traits and beliefs, which along with all the above experiences will help you continue to evolve your leadership into the highest level.

2. Visionary Leader Attribute Elements

Key visionary leadership attributes include faith and purpose. These elements provide the necessary force and drive for a person to impact their business, industry, and society. These elements combined some form of coaching and teaching allow for your career and leadership work to impact the industry and add to societal value, which is the goal in this sense of career and leadership.

Faith

I am not referring to faith here in the most understood religious terms but more so in terms of a confidence and a strong belief in yourself and your reasons for expanding your purpose in the universe. Every person's success comes from a belief in oneself and the cause (in this case I am referring to a professional cause in terms of the industry or business one is in) he or she stands for. This cause could be in terms of your passion for products or knowledge transfer or combining tools, products, and services, all for betterment of society by adding value. Of course, in the capital construct, value is measured in terms of monetary value impact predominantly. But as one thinks through it, adding value in business terms can be measured also in terms of employment-generated, sustainability efforts through new approaches and more efficient and effective ways of making products or delivering services or reducing time to do certain things in comparison to the time it took before and so on. All these ways contribute to adding value to the purpose you believe in for the greater good of society.

This faith combined with the right purpose is one of the strongest characteristics of a visionary leader. With his or her innate faith and purpose combined with the knowledge and experiences gained in the industry and field of choice, the ability to impact industry and societal change is only limited by the faith, purpose, and drive a person has.

Purpose

The elements of purpose have been described in chapter 3. It is about establishing a set of values, principles, and beliefs that give meaning to your life and then using them to guide the decisions and actions you take.

As a visionary leader, this element along with faith are key differentiators for you to have to leave a lasting impact on your legacy in terms of contributions to society from the culmination of all your work efforts in your chosen profession and industry.

There are many definitions of purpose. Many of the elements of purpose and its tie to the other elements of 5P approach has been identified in chapter 3. The key is to note that a great leader subjugates his or her ego with a deep desire for larger good through identification of purpose. This is a critical aspect in terms of evolution into this altar of leadership. It is a completely different level of thought where the act or acts of doing something for the greater good always supersedes any other thought in each of your actions, consciously or subconsciously.

Purpose and Impact

Finding purpose, defining self-purpose, and maintaining purpose is not easy. Many companies define lofty purpose statements, and their leaders are not able to articulate their self-purpose in relation to the company purpose.

Purpose is the key to navigating through the complex, ambiguous, and ever-changing world of strategy and decision-making we live in today. Very few leaders in various industries have a strong sense of purpose and even fewer can articulate their self-purpose clearly. Often, leaders interchangeably think of their organization's mission and vision as their purpose while that is not necessarily the case. Articulating your purpose and having the courage to live it is the most critical task of leadership evolution that one can undertake given the impact it can make on your life and your efforts.

Purpose-driven leadership has been written about a lot. This section is to help you understand that a personal purpose statement is critical for you to evolve your leadership to this level. As mentioned before, it is not the organization's mission or vision but your own purpose-impact statement that allows you to be true to your beliefs and challenge yourself to validate your purpose consistently by checking against it.

What does that mean?[1]

A general purpose statement could be "to make whomsoever, wherever, whenever better." This could be the purpose statement of an operations, engineering, or sales leader in an organization. An example of a purpose statement that a real-life operations director used was to "create families that excel." He created this to help keep his factory doors open during a protest movement in his country so as to enable workers who worked there to be accountable and be loyal to each other to have a sustainable living. The above purpose statement is broad and at the same time specific in its end goal as it allows for focus of the all the folks who work there, irrespective of circumstances around.

Your purpose is what makes you distinct. Whether you are a CEO or an early-stage leader or an enabler leader or an associate on a team, your purpose is your brand, what makes you tick. It's not what you do but the how and why you do it.

Purpose is not what you think it should be. It is who you cannot help being.

For example, if I had to write a purpose statement for my mother, who has always been about being there for our family and her career was as a teacher, it might read something like this, "Be there for my immediate and extended family in every small and big

---

[1]   (https://hbr.org/2014/05/from-purpose-to-impact, n.d.)

way, no matter what or where." This could be in terms of her making separate breakfasts for each of our liking while we were growing up or helping my dad with some of his crucial life decisions or accommodating our large extended family who sometimes showed up unannounced or fly all the way across Asia and Europe to be there with me at the time of a health crisis. She has always been there for the family while managing a wonderful career as a teacher and enabling the lives of many of her students. My mother cannot help being there for us as a family by either helping is with our needs or coaching us through her famous timely sayings at every instance or by preparing lessons for her students for many years.

Purpose and Action

This is the true joy in life, the being used for a
purpose recognized by yourself as a mighty one.

—George Bernard Shaw

Purpose to impact or purpose to action plans differ from traditional career development plans. They take a holistic approach toward professional and personal life and do not ignore family and other commitments. It embodies who you are as a person. After all, one cannot live every moment thinking of a purpose or any other plan, but with some thought, one can live one's life more consciously, wholeheartedly, and with more focus. Some of the elements of a purpose driven plan could include the following:

- Use meaningful career infused language
- Focus on strengths to realize career aspirations
- Create a statement of leadership purpose as to how you will lead
- Set incremental goals in achieving it
- Include your family and other elements of interest while defining your purpose

At this stage, given a reasonable degree of success in your career and all the elements that come with typical societal life, the elements of purpose should be at the forefront of your leadership thoughts and evolution. Through your industry knowledge and career, you are able to now articulate better and shape the direction of your industry toward the larger purpose you see, both for yourself and toward creating a progressive industry and increasing societal value in the space you are in. This is a continuous process of refining and honing of actions and impact toward your purpose.

Some of these actions include:

a) Listen to feedback
b) Surround yourself with positive people (this is not just at work but also around you in your daily life and in your industry connections)
c) Start conversations with new people

It is quite easy these days to spend time on our phones instead of trying to kick off conversations with people around you at various locations you may be in. People work in different fields and have varied interests. Exploring other perspectives can always spark additional elements and ideas of purpose in you. Some lateral actions to spark your purpose clarity include:

d) Explore your interests
e) Engage in what you love to do
f) Consider causes you are interested in
g) Discover what you love to do

3. Teaching and Coaching

The purpose of life is to live a life of purpose.

—Robert Byrne

Through your experiences as a leader and in your growth in understanding of various aspects of business, you would have learnt and shared various aspects of processes, products, finance, KPIs, and other aspects of business and the industry. Through your growth experiences, you would have also taught and coached your team members along the way as you put your own learning experiences into action.

At this stage in your career, your teachings from your own learning experiences and your coaching of key folks around you is critical to not only live your purpose but also allow for your purpose to be sustaining and evolving as time passes on.

It is to be noted that while there have been numerous articles and debates on the similarities and differences between teaching and coaching, it is generally accepted that while teaching is imparting skills in a certain subject to the learner, coaching is predominantly about the following:

a) Building self-belief in individuals around you
b) Unlocking their potential to act on their purpose and moving above the performance zone

As a leader, one of the key responsibilities is coaching and helping others find purpose in their lives. Our purpose is already inside of us and it is the result of that purpose that we have arrived thus far. To live our purpose, we must be able to coach and teach others to also find their purpose. This involves[2] the following:

– Allowing the folks, you are coaching, to find the quiet and ignore the daily noise to find their purpose
– Helping them understand what is unique about them that we and the others see
– Be of service with your talents, gifts, and foresight to help them see their purpose

---

[2] https://www.selfgrowth.com/articles/The_Purpose_of_Coaching.html

Chapter Thought Points: Visionary Leader Focus

- Do you feel satisfied as to where you have come?
- Has your growth in faith and purpose brought you to where you imagined?
- Have you lived by your purpose?
- Has your purpose aligned with the work you have been doing?
- Do people in your business and industry see you as a visionary?
- Have you been teaching and coaching people around you from your learned and acquired experiences?
- Are you helping shape your business and your industry with all the work that you have put in?
- Are you shaping the industry with all the experiences you have gained?
- Does your faith and purpose still resonate?
- Is your purpose impacting your industry and society around you in a manner that matches your purpose and faith?
- Do you feel fulfilled with all the above?

CHAPTER 11

Putting It All Together

If you picked up this book, my assumption is that you are either someone who is

a) wanting to grow in your career but is unsure of the path in your business and could use some clarity on the leadership elements, or
b) moving along in your career but is stuck at some point on the leadership journey, or
c) tracking along very well in your leadership journey and could use a calibration, or
d) Interested in gaining a different perspective on leadership perspectives in business.

If these are among the reasons you picked up this book, I hope you found the LQM and the 5P approach as significant takeaways for your leadership evolution understanding and evolution.

Recapping our journey thus far and putting it all together for your continued leadership evolution, we have the following:

1. Where Are You in Your Leadership Journey Today?

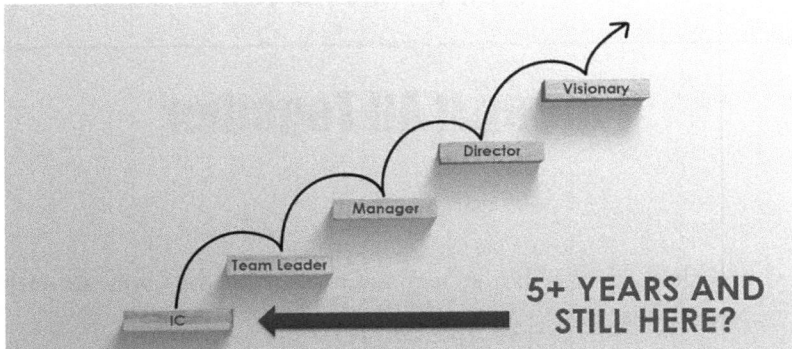

Is there a gap between where you think you should be and where you are currently at?

If the above graphic reflects the reality of your career leadership journey at any level in the trajectory shown above, it is an opportunity to reflect on the reasons for the same and make the necessary adjustments and undertake the needed learnings. Whether it is a small gap between where you think you should be or a big gap between your reality and your leadership stage and evolution in your career, reflection and action are the keys to close the gap.

2. Closing the Gap Reflections

If you conclude that there are gaps, reflect on the items below for your own situation.

- Evaluate your current skills objectively.
- Evaluate your self-awareness.
- How well do you understand why you do certain things or why you are asked to do it?

- How does what you do help the business?
- Do you tell people what to do or do you listen and learn?
- Are you able to align and influence where needed?

The chapters prior elaborate on all the above elements needed to reflect and close the gap. Reflect on each of the elements above and work on the elements needed to close the gap.

3. Reevaluating the Leadership Elements

Leadership is not control or titles or managing complexity or just performing a set of tasks. If you feel that your technical and subject skills are at their highest levels in the work you do, the gaps are most likely in the leadership elements for lack of growth. These typically include the following:

- Skill and competencies evolution
- Metrics understanding
- Workflow understanding
- Influence and Alignment abilities
- Self-awareness/relatability

Evaluate your leadership journey in a formal manner in terms of the above elements and assess yourself in terms of the direction and needs of the business and organization you are with.

4. Engagement-Impact assessment

As mentioned earlier, leadership is always about engagement and impact. Toward this, if your leadership is not where you want it to be, examine your engagement in the organization and its impact on various initiatives. There most definitely is a blind spot wherein you feel that you are working hard and pulling on many initiatives, whereas the organization may be perceiving it very differently. This requires considerable thoughtful understanding and reflection in terms of items mentioned above.

Do you feel you are good as is and are not growing in your leadership career? If so,

- are you focused just on your skills? Maybe you are a subject matter expert in engineering or marketing and doing a remarkable job at the tasks in hand but not enhancing the elements of your leadership.
- do you understand your engagement methods with your team and the adjacent teams?
- do you relate to how your work impacts others while adding value to business financials or other KPIs?
- are you able to self-reflect periodically on the impact your work, thoughts, and actions are having on your value stream and the business?
- do you understand your impact, your work's impact and how to gain alignment across your value stream and across the business?

5. Engagement-Impact Calibration

a) Reevaluate your purpose. Does it match your organization's purpose?
b) Reevaluate your self-awareness.
    a. Are you focused just on your work tasks routinely every day?
    b. Have you made any attempt formally or informally advance your skills?
    c. Do you understand your engagement with your teams in your workflow?
    d. Are you making a quantifiable and tangible impact?
    e. Can you articulate your work's wins (impact) clearly?

f. Where are you in the matrix below in the organization from the organizational perspective and from your perspective? Why?

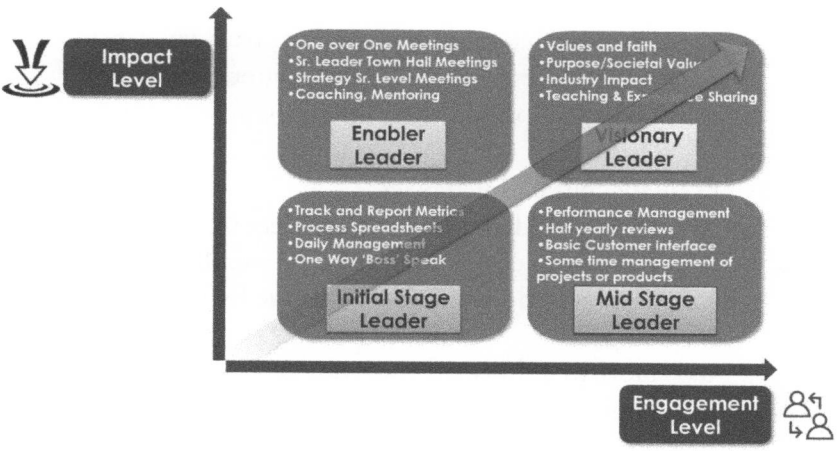

6. Tips to Reenergize your leadership journey

a) Reflect on your purpose:

Does your purpose still align with your organization's purpose? For your effective leadership growth, your purpose must continue to match your organization's purpose. Are you able to see the 5Ps clearly? Depending on the stage of leadership you are at in the organization, can you see that the right people are in the right process delivering the right products (services), and are they portable (applicable) across the organization? Do you feel that your purpose aligns with the question above, and does it match the organizational purpose? If so, reexamine the gaps and enable actions toward listed above depending on the gap. If not, then there is a fundamental misalignment in purpose, and that must be addressed.

b) Check in on your self-awareness.
   a. Can you see beyond yourself?
   b. Are you able to relate to the abilities of others?
   c. Are you curious about learning new skills and happenings in other parts of the business and the industry?
   d. Are you able to trust yourself to trust your team?
   e. Have you empowered those around you?
   f. Have you performed a self-assessment as suggested in chapter 2?
c) Evaluate your competencies.
   a. How would you rate your subject matter expertise?
   b. How well do you understand the workflow in your area?
   c. How well do you understand the fiscal aspects of your business?
   d. How well do you know your key competitors?
   e. How well do you adapt your products/services to the cultural and regional expectations?
   f. Have you improved upon your process, financial, industry, and global perspective competencies as you are progressing on your leadership journey?

Evolving Your Leadership

If I can summarize the various aspects of the book, I would suggest that one does a check-in with oneself every year and tie off with your mentors and influencers in your organization. You may have formal mechanisms for career planning in your organization, or there may be other informal ones. If you can position your conversation and leadership aspirations in terms of the three key concepts discussed in this book i.e.,

- The leadership quotient matrix
- Influencing and alignment efforts in the organization and in the industry
- Competencies growth

You will be well on your way to achieving your purpose and realizing your leadership potential and making the impact that you know you can. Remember, leadership is all about impact and engagement; and it comes about only from hard work, patience, self-awareness, and understanding besides your competencies. Hopefully, this book has given you some tangible perspectives and items for reflection and action and help you evaluate and elevate your impact.

The absolute best to you in your leadership journey!

ABOUT THE AUTHOR

Sundar Ananthasivan is an engineering management and innovation leader with leadership experience in a variety of industries. He holds a Master's degree in engineering from the University of Cincinnati and a Master's degree in business from the Kelley School of Business, Indiana University. He has two patents and has published many technical papers. He believes in a purpose-filled life and that empowerment and working to each person's strength are the keys to successful leadership and organizations. He lives in Wisconsin, USA.

CPSIA information can be obtained
at www.ICGtesting.com
Printed in the USA
BVHW031724291121
622778BV00001B/5